BATH
beyond the Guide Book

Graham Davis

REDCLIFFE
Bristol

First published in 1988
by Redcliffe Press Ltd.,
49 Park St., Bristol.

© Graham Davis

ISBN 0 948265 17 5

The main text of this book has been set in
Baskerville 11/12 point.

Photoset, printed and bound by
WBC Bristol and Maesteg

Contents

Acknowledgements

My thanks to David Flintham, editor of the Bath Evening Chronicle for kindly allowing the publication of these articles in book form.

In addition to credits recorded with the illustrations or in the text, acknowledgements are due to Avon County Library, Bath Museums Service and Maurice Temple Smith Ltd.

Cover Illustration: *The Buff Club at the Pig and Whistle, Avon Street. Robert Cruickshank cartoon c. 1825 courtesy: Victoria Art Museum, Bath.*

A lodging house in Victorian Bath's notorious Avon Street. See "Doss-House Shock Probe" story on page 59.

Introduction

This collection of pieces on the lives of ordinary people may seem singularly inappropriate for an historic city like Bath. Yet this would be to misunderstand the social history of the city where the people of Bath take centre stage.

Modern Bath was created in the late eighteenth and early nineteenth centuries when it was transformed from a small resort of fashion into a sizeable, commercial and industrial city. In the eighty years between the death of "Beau" Nash in 1761 and the opening of the Great Western Railway in 1841, the population of the city more than trebled and a dramatic expansion took place northwards from Queen Square and eastwards across Pulteney Bridge with the development of the Bathwick estate. With expansion came social segregation. Increasingly, the fashionable quarters were found on the northern slopes of the city while the former lodgings of fashionable visitors, in Avon Street, Trim Street and St. James's Parade, housed artisans and labourers. The people of Bath became segregated across a north-south divide, a process that accelerated with further expansion of the city in the nineteenth century.

To compensate for the gradual loss of the fashionable company, Bath assumed the role of a residential city. It attracted wealthy people to retire and developed its commerce and industry to support a growing population all the year round. Hence the sprouting of Georgian and Victorian suburban residences and the concentration of new industries such as brewing, printing and engineering sited alongside the River Avon and the Lower Bristol Road.

By the 1840s, industrialisation and evangelicalism had changed the moral climate. The Victorians affected to despise Georgian Bath as a "temple of frivolity" and, in selling the city as a genteel resort for the respectable middle classes, emphasised merely those aspects that suited the needs of the time — the great architectural legacy and the famous literary associations. Pleasure seeking and dissipation were discreetly left out of account. The polite world of Jane Austen rather than the unsavoury period of "Beau" Nash was preserved for posterity. The modern commercialisation of Georgian Bath has reinforced this process in the interests of promoting tourism.

Yet this narrow focus on the architectural masterpieces, adorned with house plaques in celebration of notables, who stayed however briefly, misses the vital interdependence of Bath society in the eighteenth and nineteenth centuries. The comforts provided for fashionable visitors and wealthy residents relied completely on an army of domestic servants, attendants, craftsmen and labourers who formed the bulk of the population. Moreover, the very nature of a seasonal resort attracted a host of undesirables to prey on the fashionable company — card-sharps, prostitutes, pickpockets, beggars and tramps. Not surprisingly, perhaps, there are no monuments to their activities. However, individually and en masse, they formed an unwelcome and vulgar presence in the moving stream of life on the parades, in the Assembly Rooms, at the Lansdown races and in the city streets.

So it is fitting that all conditions of men, women and children, form the subject matter of this study. Much of it is in the style and language of the day, taken from contemporary sources, not merely to reconstruct the physical conditions in which people lived but also to explore the mental pictures conjured up by observers and commentators at the time. By such means an attempt is made to get inside people's heads, to identify the fears and anxieties that guided their actions. In reading about them, we may experience a range of emotions, humour, sadness and alarm, but in doing so we may come to know ourselves a little better.

Starve 'em and Birch 'em

The first half of the 19th century saw widespread alarm about the "problem" of juvenile delinquency in Britain. Young people flocked to the towns in search of freedom, excitement and job opportunities. Industrialisation disrupted family life and hordes of orphaned or abandoned children roamed the streets. After the reform of the Poor Law in 1834, thousands of children grew up in the harsh atmosphere of the Union Workhouse and even quite young children could be sent to prison or transported to Australia.

In Victorian Bath, juveniles were constantly complained of by their elders in memorials to the Watch Committee, whether for crowding the pavements, acts of vandalism or for nude bathing:

> "Mr. Edwards and others, occupiers of shops at the Lower End of the Market Place attended the Committee and stated a great nuisance existing by the obscene and disgusting language used by girls standing on the foot & carriage way there..."

> The Memorialists "Beg to call your attention to the nuisance daily carried on by children and others congregating on the space of ground in Trinity Street and Kingsmead Square belonging to the Midlands Railway Company which is also a cause for fear to the said inhabitants from boys continually throwing stones and breaking windows. Mr. Uriah Moore of 4 Kingsmead Street claimed to have had 50 panes of glass broken!!"

> "Revd. Father Sweeney of St. John's Priory attended on behalf of himself and other residents of South Parade respecting the great annoyance occasioned by children and youths shouting until a late hour on land used as a Playground in the Dolemeads district and also by a number of youths bathing from boats and from the banks of the river in a nude state immediately fronting some of the houses of the Parade..."

Victorians deplored an offence against public morality just as much as the destruction of private property. It was commonly held that children were naturally wicked and a proper moral training required that their will be broken. Enforced hunger and physical punishment (boxing the ears and a sound thrashing with birch twigs) were the recommended means for girls as well as for boys. Despite the persistence of crime and disorder, Victorians retained a touching faith in severe punishments — hard labour, flogging, and imprisonment — as a solution to juvenile delinquency.

> A police report from the *Bath Chronicle*, 1849:
> "James White, aged 14, who from his hardihood and his
> peculations had acquired the name of 'Jack Shepherd' [a
> notorious 18th century villain], and is well known in the
> city by that distinguished title, was summoned for
> assaulting his mother, and putting her in bodily fear. The
> whole of the mother's evidence went to show how deeply
> depraved this young urchin is, as the language imputed to
> him of the most revolting nature. The daring young fellow,
> in defence, pleaded non-education, which was overruled as
> the evidence went to show that when sent to school, he
> would scale walls, or jump from the windows, so as to
> escape scholastic exercise. The bench told him that they
> should fine him 5s [25p] and in default of payment would
> gratify him with 14 days imprisonment with hard labour..."

Children brought up in the "contaminating" influence of the
Workhouse were thought to be in danger of becoming a permanent
burden on the rates. One solution was to board them out as servants
with "respectable" families. After paying a visit, Mrs. Grant reported
to the Boarding Out Committee as follows:

> "In this instance I particularly wished that Elizabeth
> Whitcombe should not go out as nurse girl: she comes of a
> very bad parentage and was old enough when first sent to
> the Workhouse to remember their evil ways: she is a fine
> handsome girl and her greatest fault is her love of dress and
> tawdry finery and I have had frequent opportunity to
> reprimand both the child and her foster parents on this
> account and I cannot but fear that all the gossiping with
> other girls when taking out Mrs. Hanham's children, and
> the being left so much to herself as all these nurse girls and
> general servants are will tell greatly to increase these bad
> propensities and ultimately lead to evil consequences."

Another solution, reported in the *Bath Chronicle* in 1849, was pauper
emigration:

> "Mr. Meredith in proposing such a scheme for Walcot,
> said he considered the parish in the position of a man with a
> large family. If a man had 12 children and small means he
> must not be too particular in the disposal of one or two of
> them. They must recollect that if this young woman
> remained here she might by and by become the mother of
> 10 or 12 other paupers... There was, however, a
> superabundance of women here, and in Australia they

were wanted . . . They did not propose to send the strength
of the country away, but the superabundant females."

I believe there may be people alive today in Bath who in their youth
were sent as pauper emigrants to Canada or to Australia. And there
are some young people, without work or prospects, who feel they are
outcasts in their own country.

A Cradle of Old Age?

In the late Georgian period the elderly were among the sick who
repaired to Bath for the waters. This was satirized by Cam Hobhouse
in a piece called "Snug Lying" from *The Wonders of a Week at Bath* in
1811:

"It sounds rather strange, but I tell you no lie,
There's many good people that come here to die;
For the London practitioners wisely declare,
When their patients can't breathe, they must try change of air.
Says Sir Walter — 'Dear Lady, I thought all the while
That dropsy of yours must proceed from the bile;
The waters of Bath have made wonderful cures
Of many I know, in such cases as yours.
You'll go down directly to Bath if you're wise.'
So down goes my Lady directly — and dies —"

At the same time Bath was gradually losing the presence of the
fashionable company that had made it the premier resort in England.

9

Something had to be done and so Bath set about persuading people to reside in the city. The *Bath Visitant* declared in 1844:

> "Of all places in the Kingdom, Bath is best fitted for the retirement of individuals with independent incomes, whether small or large. For those past the meridian in life, its quietness, beautiful neighbourhood and warmth of climate, particularly recommend it."

While Bath proclaimed its virtues to revive its flagging fortunes, outsiders cruelly exposed its faded glory. Poking fun at the elderly served to underline Bath's loss of vitality and social decline. Charles Dickens wrote to a friend:

> "Bath looked I fancied, just as if a cemetery full of old people had somehow made a successful rise against death, carried the place by assault, and built a city with their gravestones, in which they were trying to look alive, but with very indifferent success."

By the end of the century when Bath had long established itself as a genteel resort, the retired — admirals, generals, clergy and colonial servants — lent an air of old fashioned charm to the place. E. Yates wrote in *A Week at Bath* in 1891:

> "It is indeed a wonderful place of resort for very old people, of whom you see scores creeping placidly in the sunshine, or doddering about in corners sheltered from the wind... Bath and Cheltenham, taken together make up a kind of Asia Minor; so thickly do old Indians congregate at both places... There is a leisurely and conventional air about them, a tone of the invalid and dilettante. Generals and admirals abound; a perceptible portion of the inhabitants have retired from the hard work of the world. Many simply come to these places to die, and take their twenty or thirty years about it. They acquire a system or science of living; they guard against every external object that may ripple the calm stream of their lives; they deaden the force of emotions and opinions, and with noiseless calm glide over 'the rapids of life'."

From such descriptions, one would never guess that less than ten per cent of Bath's population was aged over 60. Equally, it is easy to accept the cultivated image of the city designed to attract visitors and the retired, and to ignore the plight of the aged poor. To be sure Bath was a "cradle of old age" for the comfortable classes but to be old and poor in Bath, as elsewhere, too often meant a time of dread. About a third of old people died in the Workhouse. Others faced an undignified last few days of life:

> "The evidence given at a Coroner's Inquest in 1819 on the death of an unknown woman of 70 revealed that she had come from Bristol to Bath about 4 o'clock on Thursday, January 18th and engaged a lodging for 3d per night at 57 Avon Street. She slept there on Thursday night and on Friday morning Mrs. Palmer, the lodging-house keeper, said she would not sleep there after that night. The deceased did not return until 10 o'clock on Friday evening. When she came to the house, William Palmer refused her a bed when she sat down at the step of the door. Elizabeth Palmer desired her husband to go for a Constable to remove her. John Mitchell, the watchman called to take the deceased away from 57 Avon Street but could not get her to stand. She always walked with sticks. Two other watchmen helped and they put her into a wheelbarrow and conveyed her to the Watch house and delivered her into the care of the night constable. Her clothes were very wet and dirty. She did not speak and appeared weak and feeble. They put her by the fire in the Watch house in High Street and she appeared in a dying state. She died at 1 o'clock in the morning in the presence of a surgeon. He gave his opinion that she died from infirmity of old age and the inclemency of the weather. The Coroner's verdict was death by the 'Visitation of God'."

"Paddy" Runs Amok

> "Was it not found where the Irish appeared wages were lowered, respectability disappeared, and slovenliness and filth prevailed?"

proclaimed the future Lord Shaftesbury, M.P. for Bath, speaking at the Assembly Rooms in 1848.

At a time of poverty, unemployment and political unrest, Irish migrants swelled the ranks of itinerant labour in Britain. Their utter destitution in the wake of the potato famines in Ireland made them accept the worst slum conditions in British cities, and their legendary fondness for pig-keeping in overcrowded conditions made them an easy target as undesirable immigrants. In the immediate aftermath of the famines, Irish vagrants were frequently apprehended in Bath for trying to obtain bread in bakers' shops without paying for it or called

11

"The Irish Emigrants" by John Joseph Barker, 1824–1905.
Courtesy of the Victoria Art Gallery, Bath

on the police, often it seems out of hunger and desperation to acquire a night's lodging. The *Bath Chronicle* gleefully reported "Irish" cases in the years 1847 to 1852:

> "John Williams, an Irishman and his wife, destitute and 2 children, applied to the Police Station for relief. On being searched a bottle of whisky and 10d found on them... He was discharged with a caution to leave the city immediately."

The magistrates were keen to ensure that Irish vagrants were despatched from the city, without worrying too much what happened to them once outside the city boundary.

Some of the Irish made their homes in Bath and became well known to the police. Sadly, Irish prisoners, with their all too apparent poverty, strange accents and ignorance of English ways were often the subject of amused condescension in court:

> "Mary Collins, an old Irishwoman of drunken habits, charged with stealing a waistcoat and handkerchief. The garrulity of the prisoner to her vernacular, when called upon for her defence partook of the semi-comic and excited an amusement among the bystanders which ill-comforted with her pitiful slum condition."

Comic dialogue, written in a form that pointed up an Irish brogue cruelly reinforced the stereotype of the drunken Irish:

> "An old Irishwoman, who goes by the sobriquet of 'Waterloo Poll', but whose real name is McDonald, was charged with being drunk and begging on Sunday. The prisoner said she was seized with cramp on the road from Bradford [-on-Avon], and a lady gave her some brandy. She was reminded by the Bench that she had recently been sent to prison for a similar offence.
> Prisoner: 'I hope yer worships will not send me to prison, for I should not like to die in a prison.' She was committed in default of bail to keep the peace for eight days, and in committing her, the Mayor advised her not to go on to Bristol... for it was the opinion of medical men that intemperate persons were such as were liable to the cholera.
> Prisoner: 'Why, yer worship, the docthers tould me I ought to take a dthrop of brandy to keep it away.'"

Of the 1,085 Irish-born people recorded in the 1851 census in Bath, 230 formed an Irish "colony" in Avon Street, and 38 Irish were living in one house in the street containing 58 people. Avon Street was the

13

principal lodging-house district and criminal quarter of the city. The Irish presence commanded headline treatment in the press:

> "AN IRISH ROW — John Hurley, an Irish labourer, was charged with committing a breach of the peace by fighting; and Catherine White, his wife, was charged with attempting to rescue him from the custody of the policeman.
>
> It appeared that, on Saturday night, the Police were called to quell a disturbance at the Odd Fellows Arms public-house, Avon Street, when they found from a dozen to twenty Irish, male and female, engaged in a general MELEE."

Another similar Irish incident carried the headline —

> "AN AVON STREET RIOT
> Richard Barrett, an Irishman, was charged with being drunk and disorderly in Avon Street on Saturday night.
>
> It appeared that a crowd of people were assembled before the door of the Fountain public-house, in consequence of some outrage committed by the prisoner, while he was at a window upstairs, threatening the mob outside. Presently afterwards some woman connected with him, hurled a lump of coal upon their heads. Some of the crowd, in retaliation, smashed the window when the prisoner rushed out of the house, furiously wielding a poker, and followed the people down the street, attempting to strike indiscriminately, as he proceeded. Patrick Sweeney, a labourer, with a head bandaged from recent injuries, stated that... he had not been at the door of the Fountain but a few minutes, when the prisoner took up a fender and struck him on the head inflicting several wounds, from the bleeding of which he fell to the ground insensible. He attributed the assault as an old grudge of the prisoner against him...."

By the 1860s, fewer Irish people lived in Bath and press reporting of the Irish became low key. They could no longer be blamed for slum conditions they had left behind. Today, reports of riot and disorder in our inner cities are often associated with black ethnic minorities. In the 1980s, as in the 1840s, fears about "outsiders" serve to distract attention from the real problems of housing and employment.

GUINEA
PIG-JACK
OF·BATH

A Professional Call to Alms

The tramp you may see swigging his cider on a bench in Abbey Churchyard belongs to an historic tradition. He may be an unwelcome visitor but he is one in a long line of poor travellers who have passed through the city over the centuries. Most colourful were the beggars and their notoriety was celebrated in the old nursery rhyme attributed to Bath in Grosse's *Glossary for 1790*:

"Hark, Hark! The dogs do bark.
The beggars are coming to town;
Some on nags, and some in rags,
And some in silken gown."

Of course, they were deplored by the authorities who maintained a constant vigilance against beggars deceiving the public. In the early 1800s, a report stated that "passengers were obstructed by wretches sprawling on the pavement, exhibiting mangled limbs, fictitious sores and counterfeiting convulsions, in order to extort alms." Anecdotal evidence was employed to represent a mass of trickery posing as genuine poverty. All vagrants and beggars were seen as imposters, as in the following story from Warner's *History of Bath*, written in 1801:

"A person coming down Holloway after the close of day, overheard the following between two beggars who had been plying their trade during the day in the streets of Bath.
'Well Dick what luck hast had to-day?'
'Bad: I've only touched three shillings.'
'Ah! (said the first) I've done somewhat better, here's seven and sixpence; come let's have an Alderman.'
Curiosity induced the listener to ask the meaning of the term.
'Not know what an Alderman is' was the reply, 'why it's a boiled turkey with oyster sauce.'"

If a man might receive as much from a day's begging as he could from a week's honest labour, the work ethic would be fatally undermined.

"Begging is, in truth, a regular trade," proclaimed an editorial in the *Bath Chronicle* in 1849, "a profession far more profitable than ordinary labour. A beggar said some time since, that he could go into 60 streets a day and that he thought it hard if he did not get a penny in each; he thus receives a larger sum for his idleness than is paid to skilled artisans in wages, to many classes of clerks for salaries, and even to junior officers of the army and navy, as their fit remuneration. What wonder is it that the country is swarming with beggars... when the pay is so good?"

Despite the best efforts of the magistrates, Poor Law Guardians and the police, the "problem" of beggars, tramps and vagrants reached epidemic proportions in the "hungry" forties. An estimated 20,000 of them passed through Bath each year when the population of the city was only 54,000. A policy decision in 1848 to restrict the numbers of tramps entering the Bath Union Workhouse (now St. Martin's Hospital) prompted a rebellious assault by a group of tramps who smashed the windows of the Casual Ward in a bid to be admitted for the night.

In the face of increasing numbers of travellers, the *Bath Chronicle* appealed to the public not to give alms to beggars and so dissuade them from coming to Bath:

> "The Magistrates and Guardians are still determined to prevent such an abuse of the public funds, attended as it is by no real kindness, but offering a premium to pauperism and vice, and encouraging a highly dangerous set of persons to travel over the country, passing their nights at workhouses and their days in begging, stealing, and drunkenness. There is, however, a duty which the inhabitants of Bath have to perform. It is for them to exercise discretion in the disposing of such sums as they devote to the purpose of benevolence. It is for them to remember that so long as such persons receive encouragement the evil will continue, and may again return, in all its force during the ensuing winter."

There is no recognition here of the severe economic depression of 1847–8 and no understanding that the numbers of tramps greatly increased at a time of high unemployment. The numbers reached a peak during the winter months when fewer employment opportunities existed for the labouring poor and when Bath attracted its visitors for the winter season. The latter were the target for professional beggars and thieves who arrived for the Bath season and gave all travellers a "criminal" reputation. The connection between the respectable visitors and the beggars and tramps visiting the city was not fully understood by Victorians who viewed the poor within a narrow moral framework.

Today, a similar connection operates with the buskers who are thickest on the ground on Saturdays in the main shopping streets. If I am not mistaken, their numbers have increased with the rise in youth unemployment and the fall in the value of student grants.

The following simple Remedy has been found very useful in cases of

Cholera.

Take in a table-spoonful of Brandy, as much powdered Rhubarb as will lie on a shilling.

Make a strong tea of camomile flowers, mallows, and mint, either dry or green, and take a tea-cupful frequently.

Get two pieces of wood,* each six inches square, and one inch thick, place one of them against the bars of the fire grate, or in a heated oven, till quite hot, wrap it in a flannel and lay it on the bowels. Heat one while the other is cooling.

It is strongly recommended that the above articles be procured in every family for immediate use, in case of attack of the bowels.

*N.B. If wood cannot be got, two pieces of Tile will do.

*Committee Room, Kingswood Hill,
7th January, 1834.*

God Save Us All!

Symptoms: "extremities cold... , evacuations similar to thin rice gruel, countenance excessively anxious; eyes sunk, tongue clammy, and quite cold... the patient complained of excessive thirst."

Like many other cities, Bath suffered from the first major epidemic of Asiatic Cholera in 1832. The outbreak of a killer disease in a health resort just before the winter season was regarded as bad for business so the details were kept out of the papers. As the cause of cholera was unknown and no certain cure existed, blame could be attributed after the epidemic to suit popular prejudice. R. Mainwaring's Bath Board of Health report identified drunkenness and dissolute behaviour among the poor as major factors in the incidence of the disease. Early cases were traced to parts of Bristol inhabited by the "low Irish".

> "No. 14 — Kitty Wiltshire, a poor wretched woman, aged 65, residing in Wine-Street, parish of St. James, so addicted to drinking was this poor creature, that latterly her whole time was passed in a public-house, when she could procure wherewithal to gratify the ruling passion. Here indeed was predisposition! She survived her attack 24 hours, and was buried within the prescribed time.
>
> Nos. 19 and 20 — Were two unfortunate women residing at 65 Avon-Street. Young in years, though matured in profligacy. They had been repeatedly at Bristol, during the last three weeks, and without doubt, associating in the heart of the disease.
>
> Nos. 40, 41 and 42 — Ann Payne, Ann Howell, and Rebecca Manly, residing in the immediate neighbourhood of Avon-Street... They were... habitual drunkards. Ann Howell, co-habited with Thomas Hayward, (No. 22) who died of the disease in Avon-Street; she obtained money, as compensation for the destruction of his clothes, left her house, and sought refuge in the apartment of her friend Payne, in Milk-Street. There the money was spent in liquor, and, under the influence of intoxication, these wretched women were attacked with the disease... Now mark the benevolent interposition of Providence.
>
> With broken constitutions, contracted by loose habits, and a continual course in inebriety, were these poor women attacked, with a malignant and dangerous disorder, in expectation each succeeding hour of being called to the presence of their Maker! And, yet it pleased the Almighty to spare their lives... "

With a much lower death toll than Bristol, Gloucester or Exeter, the

19

people of Bath had clearly merited the mercy of the Almighty. His wrath was directed selectively against the people of Avon-Street, where a third of the 74 cases were recorded. Unaccountably, some of these were spared.

When the cholera returned in 1849, the *Bath Chronicle* experienced some discomfort with the publicity given to the epidemic in the national press.

> "We find, in some of the country papers, a statement — 'The Cholera is raging in Bath.'... Cholera having made its appearance all over the country, it is no more than we had to expect that we should have cases here;... But they have been so remarkably few... that we have refrained from mentioning them, because we have wished to avoid creating unnecessary alarm, knowing that fear of the disease has a most powerful influence in producing it in timid and nervous persons...What then is the truth?... less than 3 deaths a week... And the deaths — few as they are — have nearly all occurred to the south of St. James's Church [now Woolworths]; so that nearly the whole of the upper part of the city, containing three-fourths of the population has been next to entirely free from the disease."

As long as cholera only really affected the lower part of the city, occupied by the poor, Bath could feel satisfied that wealthy visitors (and the trade they brought with them) would be unaffected. Complacency persisted over the need for a proper system of drainage, sewerage and above all a decent water supply for the city. Self-deception continued as once more Almighty God was thanked for "our comparative exemption from the disease" although Cheltenham had only 6 deaths from cholera in 1849 as against 90 recorded for the Bath district.

The belief in the Almighty's protection and the apparent predilection for the disease to strike only the dissolute poor provided a mental block against the adoption of preventive measures. In our current alarm about the spread of Aids, will we rely on moral condemnation of people in a "cess-pit of their own making" or will preventive measures be taken? The omens are not good.

Opposite: Bath Guildhall: target of Victorian letter writers.

Dear Editor

The letters column of the Victorian *Bath Chronicle* had its contemporary equivalents of Laurie Cahill and L. A. Partridge. If they
concealed their identity behind grand "noms-de-plumes", they were
not afraid to criticise the quality of those who presided over the city's
affairs. A failure to keep up with the times was blamed by "Justice on
the Pediment" in 1869 on the poor quality of councillors:

> "Instead of choosing garrulous old men, past real work and
> full of prejudice, or little political tradesmen, the burgesses
> should elect without preference to politics from the most
> energetic tradesmen and professional men... "

In fact, party politics was not the overriding force it is today. The
central debate focused on the future wellbeing of the city. All were
agreed that Bath's future was bound up with its function as a health
resort. What divided councillors and citizens alike was the best means
of achieving a prosperity that would benefit everyone. Should the
Town Council invest in amenities to improve the attractions of the
city, thereby attracting more visitors and more income? Or should a
policy of rigid economy be pursued, keeping the rates low, assisting
local business and attracting people to live cheaply in Bath? The
battle of the correspondence columns raged and at no time more
passionately than over the question of a corporation water supply:

> "This then is not a question that greatly concerns the
> Circus, or our crescents and squares," wrote E. L. K. in
> 1869, "but it is a very grave one for Milsom Street and
> Union Street, New Bond Street and the Market Place for
> men of business, men in trade — are they prepared, in
> shunning a sixpenny rate, to forego profits of hundreds a

21

year? In the absence of a pure and abundant water supply, and a sound drainage, it is mere trifling to suggest avenues of trees, or avenues of lamps — the pulling down a house or two here, and the widening a roadway or two there. Grant us the indispensible and useful, and then add the ornamental if you please; but unless our sanitary wants are now attended to, the decline of this city may be rapid indeed."

The failure to provide an adequate water supply was linked by "X" in 1869 with a death rate that was uncomfortably high for a health resort:

> "It has been wisely said that 'when publicity becomes dangerous to the welfare of a city, that city must be in a wretched plight, undeserving the prosperity its inhabitants are ambitious to secure.' In August 1864, *The Times* stated the death rate in Bath to be 'higher than in any other English watering place except Yarmouth... I long to see the day when Bath shall be compared not with Yarmouth, but with Swansea and when *The Times* shall proclaim through the length and breadth of England that it is the healthiest city in the United Kingdom. But this can never be so long as men continue to shut their eyes and ears, and refuse to acknowledge things unpleasant.'"

A week later, the same correspondent returned to the fray, quoting Lord Shaftesbury, a former M.P. for Bath, in favour of sanitary reform — "It is disease that is expensive, and it is health that is cheap." He argued that it was a false economy to oppose the necessary expenditure:

> "Postponement is simply evasion of duty. It is the sticklers for economy at all hazards, who oppose all expenditure, that drive visitors away and prevent others from coming... they mar the city's character for salubrity and diminish the ability of rate-payers, dependent on the city's prosperity to pay rates, much more than they diminish the rates themselves."

In reply, VERITAS championed the cause of economy, explaining bluntly that the people of Bath could not expect to be all that healthy:

> "Bath is not a place where the death-rate should be low and the wonder is that it is no higher. It is situated in a basin where there is a constant dampness and very injurious to chest infections. In addition to this, the habits and occupations of its inhabitants are not conducive to health. Among the higher classes many are addicted to

heavy dinners, to late hours, to the drinking of cheap wines (more noxious than water containing nitrates), and to the consumption of quantities of medicine. Many of the lower class live in a densely packed district with which... in point of healthiness Bethnal Green or Seven Dials would contrast favourably. From the absence of trade, the living of this class is precarious, their privations great, and their sufferings and mortality considerable."

Other correspondents joined in a lively debate, focusing on the level of rates. "Civis" rejected Bath's proposed improvements as too costly. The rates in Cheltenham were 2s 4½d in the £, Bristol 2s 5d, Clifton 2s 10d, Leamington 3s, with Bath rates at the very low level of 1s 6d in the £. The following week, these sentiments were attacked by "A Ratepayer" who claimed the comparisons were unhelpful. The other towns quoted all had growing populations, whereas the population of Bath was declining. Bath was unable to afford expensive schemes because the income available to the Corporation was low, £36,000 per annum compared with £200,000 in Bristol.

Predictably, "Civis" replied that an increase in spending had made other places more popular, thus increasing their population:

"It is to be hoped," he concluded in January 1870, "that the friends of progress will not be thwarted by the cuckoo cry of 'the poor ratepayer' but will help to make Bath in fact what she has long been in theory — 'The Queen of English Watering Places'."

In many respects the arguments continue today. Should the city council invest in better amenities — a new leisure complex, a conference centre or a science park, acting as an engine of social progress reviving Victorian municipal enterprise? Or should the wellbeing and prosperity of the city be left to private enterprise and the free market? Ironically, although Bath City Council is committed to privatisation, it is reaping the benefit today of income generated by corporation property acquired in Victoria's day.

Bad Boys in Blue

Police forces were established in the nineteenth century as full-time law enforcement agencies replacing the savage penal code of the Georgian period which included over a hundred crimes carrying the death penalty. Many of these were trivial and increasingly juries were unwilling to convict offenders. A new style uniformed police was intended to prevent crime, to protect property and to regulate an expanding urban, industrial society.

The Bath borough police force was established in 1836. Captain Carroll R.N. was appointed as the first superintendent of a force of 132 constables, 10 inspectors and 2 superintendents. This was a substantial contingent for the size of the city and an important role was assigned to the control of street activity in upholding an appropriate social tone for a genteel resort: Letter IV in the *Fussleton Letters*, 1836, contains the following verse:

"The Watchmen, too, are all dispersed,
And Bath with new Police is curs'd,
Commanded by a sturdy tar,
Who'd rule — as in a man of war —
For C----l keeps 'em all in check,
As if on his own quarter-deck,
Now — if a beggar asks a groat,
A fellow, in a smart blue coat,
Stalks up, and orders him away,
Although, perhaps, he starves that day;
For begging here a perfect trade is, —
Supported chiefly by the ladies."

To the working classes of Bath, the new police were regarded as not only an unwelcome burden on the rates but an attack on traditional freedom. A memorial to the Watch Committee in 1836 clearly stated:

"Some of us are of that Class to whom daily labour gives its daily bread: To us returning to our homes from our labours it is disgusting to see the men of this Establishment decorated in the uniform of power parading in all the insolence of idleness, and paid with our money, for walking up and down our streets, more than many of us can earn by hard and continuous toil. Let those who require protection of this expensive, insulting, and unconstitutional Guard pay for it themselves . . . "

As it turned out, neither the hopes of the propertied classes nor the fears of the labouring poor were fully borne out in practice. The police, nominally supervised by the Watch Committee of the City Council, grew in stature and independence. A military style discipline produced a high turnover of new recruits to the force. Frequent dismissals occurred for offences of drunkenness on duty or for involvement with prostitutes. Bath Watch Committee Minutes for 1836 and 1839 serve as examples:

"Mark Saunders charged with being drunk on his stand near the Talbot in St. James's Street at one o'clock in the morning with a half gallon can of beer in his possession and with being off his beat, was dismissed."

Opposite: *Sergeant Thomas Angell: a long serving police officer, 1869–93.* Courtesy of Bath Museums Service.

> "George Turner, police constable, charged with being on
> Bathwick Hill (off his beat) on the 5th June, and with
> having in an alley behind a public house in Lilliput Alley,
> assaulted a woman named Freelove Flower, is ordered to
> be discharged."

Conditions of service for the police put a premium on respectability.
Policemen were not to be seen in public houses. Compulsory
membership of the Bath Friendly Society meant regular savings was a
requirement in the force and church attendance was obligatory for
policemen when not on duty. For protection from bad company,
unmarried constables were housed in the police barracks in the
converted old gaol in Grove Street.

The respectable public image of the police concealed a degree of
petty corruption within the force. The authority of rank was abused
and constables could be intimidated into silence or their dismissal
engineered. What was reported to the Watch Committee represented
the tip of the iceberg. Most extraordinary and embarrassing was the
case involving Chief Superintendent Hughes. His unaccountable
absence in 1868 was followed by news of him residing in Taunton
Gaol on a debt charge. Certain irregularities were also reported in
connection with the sale of police clothing, for which Hughes had
been paid by two separate contractors. Further investigation revealed
that the police clerk was implicated, having demanded commission
on the sale. Hughes had also pocketed fees for the services of the Bath
Police, to which he was not entitled.

Evidence of petty corruption may partly explain the persistent
hostility of the working classes to the police — not only resentment
against interference but a sense of betrayal of the authority conferred
on the police:

> "Following the arrests of people discharging fireworks in
> London Street on November 6th 1876, it was recorded in
> the Watch Committee Minutes that, 'the mob consisting of
> 4 or 5 hundred persons resisted the Police with such effect
> that the prisoners had to be conveyed to the Police Station
> by way of Cleveland Bridge when bottles, stones and other
> missiles were freely thrown at the police whose helmets and
> clothing are damaged.'"

Conversely, middle class admiration for the police was most evident
with regard to acts of heroism and public service — stopping runaway
horses, rescuing people from the river, distributing provisions to flood
victims or acting as fire-fighters . . . the lovable British "bobby" was
an invention of the late Victorian middle class.

High Life Behind Bars

Current proposals to privatise our prisons offer parallels with Victorian prison reform. The great Victorian obsession with economy finds an echo in the present drive to reduce public expenditure at all costs. Then, as now, the ideas emanated from the United States. Pentonville was built in 1842 with single cells for the prisoners on the Pennsylvania system of enforced solitude. The belief was that solitary confinement would produce remorse in the criminal and lead to a reformation of character. Within six years of Pentonville, 54 prisons were erected on the same pattern, providing accommodation for 11,000 prisoners and the basis of our modern prison system was established. Naturally, such a programme of building was expensive and the new prisons had to be manned and maintained. Government inspectors began to compare running costs between prisons and savings on salaries were regarded as the profits of putting the prisoners to work.

A new Bath City Gaol was built at Twerton, "a little out of the Borough", as the New Gaol Superintendence Committee reported, "and in comparative quiet and seclusion will be more favourable to

Above: Bath City Gaol at Twerton after conversion to a sweet factory.

the corrective and penitential object of a gaol." The estimated cost of the gaol was £18,650 with the money borrowed from local investors to finance the building in stages. A capacity of 122 inmates was allowed for to include 20 male debtors, 12 female debtors, 10 prisoners in the Infirmary and 80 prisoners in separate cells. When completed in 1842, the cells were 13ft by 7ft by 9ft high and the Inspectors wanted the provision of a W.C. in each cell for the convenience of prisoners and to avoid inconvenience to the turnkeys. The importance attached to separation is revealed in the building plans of the architect Manners: "Evil communications corrupt good manners. In the past Prisoners have had the opportunity for exchanging histories, and have been notoriously employed in perfecting one another in habits of depredation." In addition to separate cells, there were separate yards and separate sheds for working. In the chapel, prisoners were in separate stalls only able to see the chaplain but not each other.

Mr. Pike, the Turnkey of the Old Gaol in Grove Street, was appointed as Governor of the New Gaol at a salary of £100 per annum, plus £20 for his wife acting as Matron. The Bailiff, Mr. Eldridge, testified that Pike was "active, intelligent and humane, and whether with the knowledge of his superiors or not, I think he would equally consult the interest of the City economically and otherwise." Fifteen years later, in 1857, Bath City Gaol was the subject of an inquiry by the Inspector of Prisons, Mr. Perry, who reported:

> "That the Governor has been, for several years past, in the habit of employing officers and prisoners in doing work for him in his garden, sometimes for whole days together, occasionally keeping them from chapel for the purpose; that he has employed them also in feeding and killing his pigs, in exercising, singeing and clipping his horse, in threshing his corn, in repairing his furniture, in building an ornamental fountain in his garden, and in other private services; and that the Matron (the Governor's wife) has employed convicted female prisoners, — who ought to have been engaged in picking oakum — in the performance of needlework, baby linen and crochet-work, and embroidery for herself and her married daughter."

These charges were substantially admitted and the practices complained of were regarded as "not only highly objectionable in themselves, but in direct violation of the rules of the prison." Worse still:

> "It was proved that a convicted prisoner, named Amelia Hall, one of those who worked for the Matron, had been

often allowed to partake of wine, sweetmeats, fruit and cakes, brought to the Governor's house by her friends, and it was asserted by one credible witness, that the same prisoner had been allowed to hold interviews with her friends in the Governor's house."

An especially grave view was taken of irregularities over the supply of leather required for the manufacture of shoes by the convicts. This involved a breach of contract between Her Majesty's Government and the Town Council for the maintenance of convicts in the Gaol. It appears that various fiddles were going on with contractors which operated for the benefit of the Governor and to the loss of the government. The accounts were altered to show a profit over five years when in practice shoemaking in the gaol operated at a loss. Moreover, Mr. Kitley, the schoolmaster, and Mr. Gibson, the chief warder, claimed that between 12 and 18 pairs of boots and shoes had been made for the Governor and his family in the last two years but only 11s was credited to the Governor over the same period.

As a result of the inquiry, Governor Pike was relieved of his duties. The Inspector recommended that the nominal control of the Bailiff should cease and the gaol should be in the management of the Visiting Justices. Such was the unhappy experience of the new gaol in Bath, financed by private capital, contracting for materials by competitive tender, and subject to minimal accountability. Not the best portent for the privatisation of prisons.

Girls Enticed into Life of Vice

"I was not a little astonished, as I walked through Bath, to observe the streets so crowded with prostitutes, some of them apparently not above 14 or 15 years of age,"

wrote John Skinner, Rector of Camerton in 1830. Supply and demand, rather than sin, appear to have been at the root of prostitution in Bath. Many young women were employed as domestic servants, laundresses and dressmakers — all lowly paid, seasonal work and easily open to exploitation. These were just those occupations from which prostitution recruited most successfully. Girls from the country districts coming to Bath in search of employment and excitement, were easy prey to those with offers of lodgings and pretty clothes who could entice them into a life of vice.

The Buff Club at the Pig and Whistle, Avon Street. Robert Cruikshank cartoon c. 1825.

Information concerning Vagrants provides the following examples in 1823 and 1825:

> "Sarah Holding saith she has no means of getting her livelihood and that she walks the streets by night and is a common prostitute in the parish of St. James'."

The "Girls of the Town" plied their trade in the places of public amusement and recreation — along the parades, in Victoria Park and at the Theatre Royal:

> "William Culliford, Patrole: in St. Johns Court adjoining the Playhouse about 10 o'clock on 20th, Louisa Hulbert and Mary Ann Elmes, single women, well known as common prostitutes, wandering abroad and making a great noise and disturbance, collecting a crowd about them and wantonly taking off the hats of the persons then and there passing, and being both intoxicated with liquor... "

Public houses were also important centres of prostitution where the girls could meet potential clients and some landlords made upstairs rooms available by arrangement. In the mid-century, the Bath Police had a list of 15 disorderly pubs, considered as the known haunts of thieves and prostitutes. Normally the police took the view that it was better not to disturb the practice and drive it underground by prosecution. In the 1880s, an action by the Revd. W. J. Bolton,

Rector of St. James's, against the landlord of the notorious Bell Inn succeeded in the licence being withdrawn. In protest, the landlord claimed that Bolton's anti-vice campaign had lost him £400 in takings. The Bell Inn was at the entrance to St. James's Court, within a few yards of Bolton's parish church, where he found a nest of brothels, with upwards of 60 prostitutes, encouraging each other in drunkenness, debauchery and profanity:

> "By day, even on Sundays, and within a stone's throw of
> St. James's Church, dissolute women, half-dressed, would
> stand in groups, soliciting passers-by. At night, riots,
> fighting and piano playing disturbed the whole neighbour-
> hood. Respectable people were ashamed to live in or pass
> through such a district.'

Interestingly, Bolton received little support for his campaign, either from the police or from the City Council. His suggestion that the Council should buy up the houses of ill-repute in St. James's Court and convert them into much-needed artisans' dwellings was rejected. The sacred rights of property were at stake. Ironically, this view was shared by a brothel-keeper charged before the magistrates and reported in the *Bath Chronicle* in 1863:

> "Giles Cliff, keeper of an improper house, was brought up
> charged with being drunk and riotous and assaulting the
> police, and fined 5s and costs. On this decision being made
> known to him, he very coolly told the magistrates that he
> could easily pay that, and before going out of the room
> addressed them in the following words: 'If either of you
> gentlemen patronize my house, I will put an extra 5s on to
> you to get this back again.'"

The magistrates, in their wisdom, called the prisoner back before the bench, and altered the earlier sentence to one of a fortnight in gaol. Of course, it was illegal to keep a disorderly house, although prostitution itself was not a criminal offence. Nevertheless, prostitutes frequently indulged in criminal activity on their own account, as the *Bath Chronicle* reported in 1845:

> "Mary Ann Rose, a prostitute, was charged with picking
> the pocket of Wm. Sheppard, of a sovereign and some
> silver. The evidence was sufficient to send the prisoner for
> trial, but Mr. Blathwayt, the committing Magistrate, told
> the prosecutor, that his own conduct in the affair had been
> so discreditable that he was not likely to be allowed his
> expenses for the prosecution."

Among potential clients of the "Girls of the Town" were visitors to

Bath, local farmers staying overnight for market days, hauliers from Radstock selling their coal and regiments of soldiers camped outside the city. Counting the girls on the streets and others operating from disorderly houses, not forgetting the brothel-keepers and publicans also involved, there were probably several hundred people dependent on the business of prostitution in Bath. Annual turnover must have run into thousands of pounds. If that is the case, it ought to be recognised as an important service industry. It is a reminder, too, that however outwardly respectable Victorian Bath pretended to be, "it never quite forgot its old dissipation".

The Long Arm of the Law

As Victorian England became an increasingly urban society so its people became subject to greater legislation and control. The tide of legislative reform involved closer regulation, frequent inspection and an inevitable interference into areas hitherto free from outside control. This loss of traditional freedoms took place at the place of work, in the public streets, in working class leisure pursuits, and even between husband and wife, parents and children. Many of the conflicts arose over differing sets of values between legislators on the one hand and those on the receiving end of the new regulations, who had yet to be convinced of the need to lose their old freedom from interference. The following examples, spread throughout the Victorian period, illustrate the range of petty regulations that encroached on the lives of ordinary people:

> "Emma Rose was charged with causing an obstruction in Southgate Street on Monday afternoon, by placing a basket of fish near the footway. Fined 1/- and costs or 3 days.
>   The Mayor observed that the Bench were determined to repress the use of obscene language that now prevailed in some parts of the city."

> "William Hood, landlord of the Bacchus beer-house, Corn Street was summoned for allowing gaming on his premises."

> "Edward White, Chemist, 19 Kingsmead Square, summoned for having neglected to have his child vaccinated. The defendant said the child was far from healthy and he would have it vaccinated when well enough. It was stated that the defendant did not believe in vaccination. The defendant said he was misunderstood."

A School Board Inspector doing the rounds.

All these cases ostensibly dealing with very different offences were united by the common element that they involved new encroachments on traditional freedoms. It is little wonder that rather more than passive resistance was used on occasions when new regulations were enforced against individuals. External authority, in whatever guise it presented itself, was liable to be met with sullen resentment, verbal abuse or even violent assault:

> "George Pickford and a married woman named Maggs
> were summoned for threatening to assault George Batt.
> The parties live in the neighbourhood of Milk Street, and
> the complainant having got a distress on the premises
> occupied by the defendants for the arrears of ground rent,
> he was assailed furiously by their tongues. Case dismissed
> on the promise of good behaviour."

An example of the persistence of a cultural conflict between the legislators and those who saw themselves as victims of new and unwanted regulations occurred with the compulsory enforcement of school attendance after the 1870 Education Act. A City of Bath bye-law in 1878 enforced school attendance on all children aged between 5 and 13 unless the child had reached the 5th standard prescribed by the code of 1876. This edict struck at the heart of traditional parental freedom. It was also a serious financial blow to many poor families dependent on child earnings. Compulsory school attendance not only meant that these were lost but an extra expense had to be found to pay for schooling itself. A hard core of truancy offences had the effect of doubling the total number of petty offences committed in the city. The new legislation had created a new breach of the law that functioned on a large scale.

Predictably, a disproportionate share of prosecutions were directed against the poorest areas of the city. Prosecutions against parents for not ensuring school attendance of their children was only the beginning of a protracted process. The offenders were usually fined 1/- to 3/- for each offence or 3–5 days in gaol. Invariably, the mother appeared in court with the father at work or having left home. Repeat offences were depressingly common. Boys in work could earn a 1/- a day or the equivalent of a fine. Persistent truants were deemed beyond parental control and sent to Industrial Schools in Bath. The parents were legally obliged to pay towards their upkeep inside the Industrial School. This completed the circle of absurdity. Poor families kept children away from school, either as child minders to release the mother for work or as earners themselves. Increasing financial penalties for truancy offences undermined the fragile household economy of the poor. A system of regular payment took no account of the uncertain nature of casual earnings, so payments fell into arrears. Unable to meet them, families broke up or left the district.

Hard core poverty and illegal juvenile employment acted as counterweights to the efforts of the School Board. Dickensian conditions of cruelty and appalling neglect of children, some even sleeping rough in the market at night, can be documented at the turn of the century. As late as 1901, the census report estimated that 209 boys and 80 girls were employed illegally in Bath. And in 1902 a local H.M.I. made this despairing comment on indifference to the value of elementary schooling:

> "Ambition to improve themselves either mentally or financially seems to be dormant among the class that form the bulk of the population."

Today, we might pause to consider why truancy from school and illegal juvenile employment in our inner cities is now returning to levels only previously seen in the late Victorian period.

When Fun City Turned to Faith

Have you ever noticed just how many Victorian churches there are in Bath? These very often splendid buildings embody not merely a variety of architectural styles but are supreme monuments to an avowedly religious age. And by any standards Victorian Bath was a formidably devout city. In the 1851 Religious Census, Bath was one of the few cities to have adequate accommodation for all its citizens at a place of worship. It had one of the highest levels of church attendance recorded anywhere in the country and every kind of religious denomination was represented among its churches and chapels. It was blessed with numerous religious societies and religiously inspired charities of every description. In this period, too, Bath was well known for its preachers such as the Revd. Tottenham who "held large concourses spellbound by his devotional rhetoric" and the widely acclaimed William Jay, the dissenting minister of Argyle Chapel. Yet religious enthusiasm did not command universal support, as the pamphlet, *Lud Hudibras*, reported in 1840:

> "The clergy of this town by their preaching and ex- hortations have endeavoured to suppress the various amusements of the place, and indeed so comprehensive have been their denunciations, that scarcely an enter- tainment of a publick character has escaped; concerts, balls, races, theatrical exhibitions, and even horticultural shows, have each of them been the subject of clerical vengeance."

The same author not only blamed the clergy for the decline in the

St. Michael's Church, Bath.

number of visitors to Bath but accused them of "narrow-sited bigotry" and of fierce denominational rivalry. Whereas frivolity and indulgence epitomised Georgian Bath, the city eagerly donned the mantle of moral earnestness characteristic of the Victorian age.

Religiosity was rampant, but while church and chapel competed for financial support from the religious community in building schools and places of worship, the battle for the allegiance of the working classes in Bath was quietly being lost. All kinds of heroic efforts were made and in the long run all proved of no avail. More generous free accommodation was provided in many churches like St.

36

James's in the 1840s to fight "crime and immorality which must abound where even the ordinary advantages of church accommodation possessed in every parish are wanting". Sadly, free seats proved insufficient incentive to attract the urban masses. A more positive move was to take religion into people's homes. The Bath City Mission reported in the *Bath Chronicle* in 1887:

> "The empty benches in our churches and chapels showed the need of such a society; for many who, while they lived in the country, went to their place of worship, when they came into the city dropped out of the ranks..."

Reference was also made to

> "a spirit of indifference and in the case of some, active opposition to the claims of the Gospel".

A way of reaching young people was to provide a regular round of social activities. The Methodists offered the Band of Hope, Girls and Boys Parlours, weekly walks and occasional outings or "treats", in addition to religious events, to bring in recruits. A drive to enlist adults involved 10 day missions, harvest festivals, and taking to the streets, as the Report on the Milk St. Mission in 1899 revealed:

> "During the summer... open air preaching has been vigorously carried on, principally in Milk Street, but sometimes in Avon Street and Corn Street, with the valuable assistance of the New King Street Mission Band. Many persons have professed conversion during the year, most of whom continue in fellowship with us to this day."

The optimistic tone was misplaced. While a few converts were made to the cause of religion, religious institutions remained a target for the disorderly boys in the neighbourhood. Complaints were made in the *Bath Chronicle* in 1887 that the windows of Milk Street Chapel were constantly being broken and of disruptions caused to religious services:

> "A deputation from the Teachers conducting a Sunday School in Milk Street... complained of the inconvenience they sustained by reason of the disorderly conduct of Boys and others making noises on Sunday afternoons and disturbing the neighbourhood. It was decided that a Constable should be stationed in Milk Street from 2.30 to 5 pm on Sunday afternoons."

New religious organisations like the Salvation Army found active opposition not only from its rivals but also from local residents.

Having had its meetings in Newark Street barracks broken up by hired rowdies, the Army was met with further disruption and complaint about its street services, as reported in the Watch Committee Minutes in 1887:

> "A memorial was read from the inhabitants of Kingsmead Square calling the attention of the Authorities to the disgraceful scenes there on Sundays caused by the Salvation Army and other denominations congregating there."

Respectability and religion went hand in hand. The poor who were struggling for survival in this world were suspicious of the promise of salvation in the hereafter. Louie Stride, a child of the Edwardian slums of Bath, and author of *Memoirs of a Street Urchin*, provides an explanation:

> "I don't know how I came to be inveigled into going to Sunday School as I had no belief in God. My mother had taught me prayers very early, and I always said 'Gentle Jesus' before I slept, but it wasn't real. How could there be a God when I was always so hungry, and when I had prayed so hard in former days, and no food turned up, unless I pinched it?"

The Demon Drink

Does moral exhortation change individual behaviour? Can Parliament legislate to alter the conduct of the nation? Both methods persist today as in the Victorian past in dealing with the problem of alcohol abuse.

The Temperance Movement began in the 1830s and in a religious age became one of the great crusades of the century. Drinking was deeply entrenched in popular culture at all levels of society. The wages of working men were commonly paid, by arrangement with the landlord, in a public house. Heavy consumption of liquor formed a test of manhood among all social classes and the expression "drunk as a lord" was rooted in upper class behaviour. As the decadence and frivolity of the Georgians gave way before the moral earnestness of the Victorians, temperance posed as the champion of all the social virtues against the evils of the demon drink.

Victorian Bath was a resort of pleasure and was renowned for its brewing industry and host of public houses and taverns. It was also a city captured for a time at least by religious zealots. So it was natural

Temperance propaganda pulled no punches.

that the several Temperance Associations waged a crusade against public houses in the city:

> "Experience shows," a memorial claimed in 1867, "that poverty, immorality, and crime are in proportion to the facilities afforded for the sale of spirituous liquors. That in the city and borough of Bath, while there are 74 bakers shops, 51 butchers shops, there are within the same area 300 places for the sale of intoxicating drinks — not just for public convenience but in many instances are the haunts of the idle and dissipated to the serious injury of public morals."

Col. Blathwayte in reply to the memorial argued that

> "the pest was the beerhouse. In the common alehouses the master and man met together — the master behaved himself in order to keep up his dignity, while the man was ashamed to misbehave himself before his master. But, in these wretched places — beerhouses — there were no such influences, and poaching, felony, and crimes of every description were hatched."

Much of Temperance propaganda was in the form of tracts,

pamphlets and songs. A star turn at Temperance meetings was the reformed drunkard who would crudely and comically regale his audience with lurid stories of his former life under the evil influence of drink. A common theme was that drink was a major cause of the poverty of many families. Whether drink formed a sixth of working class budgets, as the social investigator Rowntree calculated in 1901, there is no doubt it consumed too high a proportion of low incomes, leaving insufficient for the barest essentials. A husband's excessive drinking invariably meant a hungry wife and children. They learnt to steal or go hungry, and so began a vicious circle of drink, poverty and crime. Pubs themselves were commonly associated not only with disorderly behaviour but in notorious cases were the focus of criminal activity. Thieves, swindlers and prostitutes were known to congregate in certain pubs in Bath. To establish a better image, a number of Temperance Hotels, including the Fernley Hotel in North Parade, were opened, along with other rival establishments selling hot cocoa, but they never posed a serious challenge to pubs and hotels selling alcohol.

Frequently anecdotal evidence was employed to point up the lowering effect on family life of unwise expenditure on drink. The Revd. Whitwell Elwin, chaplain to the Bath Union Workhouse, complained in 1842 that men earning high wages were often the worst offenders:

> "I was lately informed by a master tailor of Bath that one of his men, who had earned £3 a-week at piece work for years, had never within his knowledge possessed table, chairs, or bedding. I found the statement on examination to be strictly true. Some straw on which he slept, a square block of wood, a low three-legged stool, and an old tea-caddy, are the complete inventory of the articles of a room, the occupier of which, with only himself to maintain, was wealthier than many in the station of gentleman. He had frequently excited lively compassion in benevolent individuals, who supposing that he was struggling for very existence, furnished him with a variety of household goods, which were regularly pawned before a week was out, and afforded to the observer fresh evidence of the extremity of his distress. The cause of all this is quickly told. The wife was to be seen going to and fro several times a-day with a cream-jug of gin and to gratify this appetite, they had voluntarily reduced themselves to the condition of savages."

Although suspect, this kind of evidence genuinely reflected popular feeling against the social consequences of heavy drinking. Nationally, beer consumption per head of population reached a peak in the 1870s. Locally, the number of offences of drunkenness fell from 242 in 1852 to only a quarter of that total by the 1880s. Despite the increase in the number of teetotallers, moral exhortation probably had little effect on the nation's drinking habits. More significantly, the Licensing Act of 1872 which was opposed by the Temperance Movement, was followed by a decline in the number of publicans' licences and a levelling off in drink consumption for the rest of the century.

As is widely known, our modern licensing laws date from the munitions crisis during the First World War. A shortage of shells for the frontline was put down to drunkenness among munitions workers. To remedy the crisis, opening hours were limited, the alcoholic strength of beer was reduced and the price of a pint was raised sharply through taxation. Not only did this contribute to victory but equally important the old Victorian levels of drinking declined steadily as people turned to other forms of consumption. The reversal of these trends in recent years has made the abuse of alcohol once more a major social problem.

A Moral Duty?

Before the creation of the Welfare State and twentieth-century levels of income tax, the rich used to give money to the poor through the agency of charity. Older charities, dating from the Middle Ages, were part of a Christian tradition of alms for the poor. The spectacular growth of charities in the first half of the nineteenth century reflected a more secular outlook and a more positive ambition. It was no longer thought enough to meet the needs of the downcast, now the aim was to raise them up through moral improvement.

Bath was endowed with numerous charities which had to cater for the needs not only of the resident poor but also had to assist the huge influx of poor travellers who annually visited the city — an estimated 20,000 in the 1840s. This was a problem that, as the *Bathonian* reported in 1849, could produce "the most painful reflection which can occupy the contemplative mind of the visitor to our beautiful city, the strong contrast presented by wealth and poverty... which threatens ere long to be of serious impact to the wellbeing of its inhabitants."

The Monmouth Street Society, which helped travellers passing through the city, proclaimed that its charitable activities promoted social harmony:

Lord Shaftesbury who, as Lord Ashley, served as M.P. for Bath 1847-51.

"Systematised charity, as practised by the Society, may be expected to create more kindly relations between the richer and poorer classes, each benefitting the other by mutual re-agencies of good sympathies and good exertion, and then to advance through all gradations of rich and poor, the general welfare of the community."

This was an idealized view of charity in action. The reality was that with the cost of relief estimated at £10,000 annually and with economic stagnation in the city, it was difficult to raise sufficient charity for the poor. This did not deter Lord Ashley, the future Lord Shaftesbury, M.P. for Bath, the famous philanthropist and social reformer, from reminding wealthy people of their moral duty. Bath, he argued, should be a model city for subjects of philanthropy and "in proportion to their wealth, so ought to be their exertions" (a form of voluntary income tax). Ashley knew enough not to limit his appeal to noble instincts but to exploit the anxieties of the propertied classes in 1848, the year of revolution throughout Europe:

> "With a population in its present degraded state," the *Bath Chronicle* reported, "he saw no security for the internal peace of the realm... And of this he was sure, that if we remained in apathy, and put not our shoulders to the wheel to remove the evils which had been discovered we could not hope to be considered in the sight of God as a wise and understanding people."

The particular occasion of his speech before a large gathering of councillors and clergymen in the Assembly Rooms was the inaugural meeting of the newly-formed Baths and Laundries Society, established to provide washing and bathing facilities for poor families of whom many lived in single-room accommodation:

> "Thus hundreds and thousands never saw the comfort of a change of linen, and became so habitually filthy as to be unable... to appear in any place of worship (Hear, hear)... To what purpose was it to say to them not only 'be ye warmed, and be ye clothed,' but 'be ye clean, and be ye decent,' if we witheld from them the means of warmth and clothing, and the common necessaries for cleanliness and decency? Wealth and power must lend their influence to render the people fit to receive the ministrations of the clergy... "

Situated at the bottom of Milk Street in the heart of a poor district, the Baths and Laundries were not without success, but not in the way that was intended. *Bodies and Souls*, a pamphlet written in 1864, describes its activities. When the superintendent, Mr. Cox, was asked whether the poor used the baths, he replied:

> "Never — our bathers are chiefly mechanics, shop girls from Milsom Street, and domestic servants. Not at all the class for which the place was started. They won't come. It's a great pity."

The urban poor were not easily seduced by offers of charitable assistance, finding the price of dependence and conformity too high. The refusal of charitable aid and of the religious values associated with it represented a form of social protest by the working classes. The point was made most forcibly in a Chartist poster, addressed to the poor of Bath in 1841:

> "But what do you suppose will be resolved upon to allay your miseries and improve your condition? Will it be

endeavoured to remove THE CAUSE of your distress?...Or your unjust exclusion from your NATURAL RIGHTS the enjoyment of which would protect you and render you prosperous and happy? No! It will be agreed to raise a subscription by which a few loaves of bread and baskets of coal may be doled out among you — CHARITY will be extended to a small degree, but JUSTICE WILL BE DENIED. Now you should understand this important fact — if JUSTICE WERE DONE YOU, THERE WOULD BE NO NECESSITY FOR CHARITY."

Eventually, the Chartists' plea for the right of working men to have the vote was granted. The existence of Child Poverty Action Group, Shelter and Age Concern, and an estimated expenditure of ten billion pounds a year on charity in Britain prompts the question whether the vote was enough to secure the Chartist vision of social justice.

Bastille Days of the Workhouse Test

Arguments over the cost of the unemployed, the sick and the aged are by no means unique to our own time. The reform of the old poor law system in 1834 was an attempt to reduce the burden of the poor rates by encouraging greater self-reliance among those in receipt of poor relief. The framers of the Poor Law Amendment Act were confident that pauperism could be eradicated by making life uncomfortable for the able-bodied pauper and discriminating against the "undeserving" poor. Under the new system, those seeking relief were to be confronted with the "workhouse test" — enter the workhouse or go without relief. Dubbed as "bastilles" by the poor for their resemblance to prisons, the early Victorian workhouses were intended to be places of dread with a powerful stigma attached to all who entered them.

To justify the new severe system of poor relief anecdotal evidence was produced to cast the poor in a bad light. A leading exponent of this art was the first chairman of the Bath Board of Guardians and a strong advocate for the new poor law, the Revd. Thomas Spencer. Spencer was clear that the evils of pauperism had to be attacked. There was no room for misguided sentiment especially with regard to aged paupers:

"Leaving out as exceptions, the afflicted and bedridden," he wrote to the Poor Law Commission in 1836, "the

44

The women's yard in a Union Workhouse.

characteristics of the aged pauper are dirty and intemperate habits; begging and stealing to add to his parish
pay; a discontented spirit, the result of an ill-spent life.
Wherever he goes, he affords a living demonstration that
youth may be profligate and manhood improvident, and
yet old age be equally well provided for at the public
cost."

Arguing that the payment of outdoor-relief provided the opportunity
for paupers to obtain additional income from charitable sources, he
wrote in a pamphlet in 1838:

"In this idleness it becomes a great source of amusement to
devise schemes of extracting money from private bene-
volence. Ladies of leisure, with no knowledge of the habits
of the poor, and with more kindness than discretion, visit

45

such persons: they conceal from them all favourable facts, and detail only such as are likely to obtain pity and a donation; they receive good clothing, which, if they wear, would prevent the next visitor from helping them — therefore, they pawn it, and turn it into gin. They are then ready for fresh presents of clothing and money; they will always put on the appearance of rags, want, and wretchedness, by day, for these are the wares they deal in — this is their horrible trade; and in the evenings, when their benefactors have gone home, they commence their mirth and festivity."

As chairman of the Board of Guardians, Spencer had supervised a reduction in the poor rates from £19,928 to £11,520 amid much criticism and controversy and in the following three years poor law expenditure in the Bath Union rose again to £14,180. Spencer defended the interests of poor ratepayers and berated the Board for bowing to popular pressure:

"they have taken the smooth, the downhill course of complying with the desires of all that were formerly discontented... In their desire to be thought compassionate, they overlook the thousands of burthened ratepayers, respectable widows with small incomes, tradesmen with large families, young men setting up in business, all of whom, by a little increase in their taxation, would be ruined."

Public attention in Bath centred on the Board of Guardians' treatment of Ann Perry, a bedridden octogenerian, who was supported by a widow with four children, named Mary Price. Her case was championed by A. G. Barretté in a pamphlet written in 1837:

"The poor woman, who is upwards of eighty years of age, and infirm in the very greatest degree, has always borne an unexceptionable character. For these ten years past, she has been lodged and fed out of mere compassion by a widow named Mary Price, who, during her husband's lifetime, was able to do so without detriment to her family, but since his death about four years since, has become reduced in circumstances. Ann Perry was afraid of applying to the parish, lest by doing so, she would be forced into the Workhouse, and Mary Price also."

Eventually, Price applied for out-relief on behalf of Perry, who was ordered by the Guardians into the workhouse. An appeal was made to the magistrates who ordered the Board to grant out-relief to Perry. Two of the Guardians then visited Price and persuaded her into withdrawing her application. Finally, under pressure from a long-awaited ruling by the Court of King's Bench, the Guardians relented and out-relief was granted to Ann Perry. While the magistrates and Guardians argued over issues of high principle, while appeals to justice and humanity poured forth unabated, Ann Perry the victim, died the same month relief was granted.

Behind the public rhetoric on behalf of the beleaguered ratepayers or compassion expressed on behalf of the poor lay a power struggle for control of poor law expenditure between the magistrates and the Guardians. Today's politicians play the same game — posing as champions of the taxpayers or as friends of the unemployed. Those who care most passionately about holding power might be least suited to exercise it dispassionately.

Simply Charming, My Dear

Much has been written of the "new woman" of the 1860s, throwing off the suffocating restrictions of Victorian domesticity and challenging the feminine ideal prescribed in a patriarchal society. We are all familiar with those spirited, pioneering women who carved out a career outside the family to give inspiration to thousands of unknown Victorians. The work of Florence Nightingale in the Crimea, Josephine Butler crusading against licensed prostitution and Mary Kingsley exploring Africa, were representative of a great achievement by formidable Victorian women.

They were, of course, the exception and, although a stirring of women's consciousness took place in late Victorian society, it is doubtful whether more than a small minority of women subscribed to the idea of "women's rights". More traditional values remained predominant.

A glimpse at the social calendar in Bath in the closing years of the century selected from Penelope's Diary in the *Bath and County Graphic*, records a greater physical and intellectual freedom than a generation before but the overwhelming emphasis is one of crushing social conformity.

> "February 19th — A hockey match between the Clifton High School and the Bath High School, resulting, I am sorry to say, in the defeat of the home team by 7 goals. Tea was afterwards dispensed at Portland Place, and, perhaps, afforded some consolation to the defeated."

Apeing the sporting endeavour of Eton and Rugby, the girls'

47

boarding schools that sprang up from the 1870s greatly extended opportunities for physical endeavour. And in enjoying hockey, lacrosse and rowing, young ladies probably shocked their grandparents brought up on strict notions of female frailty. Penelope's light-hearted tone in the reporting of girls' hockey was repeated on the hitherto earnest subject of a religious lecture:

> "March 4th — Talking about lectures, it is not often one sees the Museum so full as it was on the occasion of the Revd. A. V. Magee's lecture on 'Science and Faith'. With the genial Canon Quirk in the chair, and the elegant lecturer at the desk, the evening passed only too quickly, and very few will forget the interesting and, at many times, humorous discussion which followed."

An event that required one's presence out of social duty could turn out happily. Making a social event out of a moral obligation was a characteristically Victorian practice.

> "June 7th — The gardens of Vellore, now the property of the Bath College, are all that can be desired for a garden party, and the one given by Mrs. Yorke-Fausset in aid of the Royal Victorian Home for Women was very enjoyable. The weather was perfect, and tea under the spreading branches of a huge old cedar was very refreshing. Tables were dotted about the grounds bearing basket work made by the inmates of the Home, which is for the reception and treatment of inebriates and other cases. It is actively supported by the Duke and Duchess of Beaufort, the Duchess of Bedford, the Countess of Dudley, Lady Battersea, and many other ladies.

Penelope took a keen interest in the decorations at social events, which were invariably described as "charming", and lovingly recorded the details of what everyone was wearing.

> "October 27th — The Prince of Mayors, as he has been aptly described, welcomed his guests with such a hearty handshake, and the Mayoress surrounded by many friends in the dais charmingly decorated with flowers, took much interest in all that was going on. Mrs. Simpson had on a dress of that pretty soft shade of pink so much worn, draped with flowers of Point-de-Flandres. Her ornaments were diamonds and pearls. Her beautiful bouquet composed of pink and white flowers was placed with the mace and insignia of office on a table in front of the vestibule. Dancing commenced at ten o'clock to the strains of the bands of Mr. Max Heymann and Herr Schöttler in the

Mrs. Woodiwiss, Mayoress of Bath, in her finery.

49

Pump Room and Concert Room. Whilst the rooms were thus engaged the Museum and Roman Promenade afforded welcome retreats; the latter, I think, looked better than I have ever seen it, the festoons of lamps, combined with the lanterns, gave a charming effect... Some of the dresses were very pretty. Miss E. Marshall was gowned in white moiré, with silk trimmings... Miss Spender wore a soft blue silk with very long train and long sleeves, a style which suited her slight figure; then the Misses Cary looked exceedingly well in a rich white satin, relieved by very little trimming, well adapted to their height and figure. But really there were so many pretty dresses and so many attractive faces that I could not help wondering why so many partners were smoking in the promenade instead of dancing... I daresay, being an ancient Grecian maiden, I may be behind the times, but in my young days Apollo never smoked in the presence of Venus."

No doubt those singled out for their appearance enjoyed a warm glow of satisfaction but the detailed description of dresses and decor suggests Penelope was writing for a wider female audience. Those who were never invited — that army of genteel poor who found a sanctuary in Bath — yet took pleasure in reading about who was there. The more glittering the occasion, the greater the compensation for their own reduced circumstances.

"November 30th — The Revd. E. Handley and Mrs. Handley gave a recherché dinner at their residence in the Royal Crescent. Eighteen guests were present, including Lord and Lady Temple, Lady Mary Skrine, Lady Eva Heathcote, and other distinguished friends. The youthful bride of the evening, Mrs. Delavel Astley, had the place of honour by Lord Temple; she looked, so everybody said, most lovely in a white satin frock relieved by blue chiffon.

The table was decorated with choice orchids grown by Mr. Handley. The table centre was brilliant, being interspersed here and there with miniature gems, which scintillated and reflected every ray of light. The chef was specially engaged from town, so that the viands and the good wine satisfied the most fastidious tastes."

Paradoxically, the brittle gaiety of the social calendar was sustained in the public eye by the admiration and deference of genteel ladies who, although frequently single, remained wedded to traditional social values.

Sales of the Century

The recent closure of a number of retail businesses of long standing in the city — Mitchells, Shutters, and The Red House Bakery — is a reminder that shops not only form familiar landmarks but represent an important part of our local history. From Victorian times retailing experienced a revolution that created the modern household names in our high streets. The commercial modernisation of shopping, based on advertising, competitive pricing, cash sales and a fast turnover of stock, was to launch the founding of department stores and multiple retail outlets such as Liptons and Sainsburys. Most significantly, the multiples brought shopping within the experience of ordinary people.

Victorian Bath was a major regional shopping centre catering for the luxury end of the market. A magazine article written in 1887 rejoiced that:

> "The shops of Bath are a revelation to the stranger, and give token of the fact that Bath is still the centre of fashion and luxury not only to the fashionable visitors, but to the whole of the West of England. Kings of Milsom Street would do credit to the Rue de Rivoli or Regent Street, for sustained splendour and gorgeous raiment."

The high class shops were evidence of the refined taste of its citizens and proved attractive to visitors in providing the further benefits of economy and civility.

> "The tone of a city can generally be ascertained from the character of its shops," purred the author of *Bath Miscellanies*, "in Milsom Street we see at once that Bath is entirely a place of 'genteel' resort and independent residents. The perfumers, milliners, tailors, printsellers, circulating libraries etc., which occupy the principal streets, proclaim it a city of easy and elegant life."

One satisfied customer delighted in Bath's "refined society, where elegance and taste are the rule, vulgar show the exception... my table is cheaply supplied, and of the best, traders uniformly civil, obliging and fair."

All this applied to wealthy residents and visitors but for most of Bath's citizens shopping scarcely existed as we know it. At mid-century, it was a much more humble affair, more in keeping with the East End of London than the graceful "Queen of the West". Compare Milsom Street with this description, from Adrian Ball's

51

52

Yesterday in Bath, of the Market Place on a Saturday night in 1849:

> "Itinerant vendors of almost every class of article for household purposes took their stand on each side of the street. Some — especially the retailers of Staffordshire ware, such as pans and pitchers — laid out their stock on the ground, as also did the vendors of vegetables and greens. These always pitched their stalls on the Guildhall side of High Street. Others converted their barrows into stands, on which all kinds of articles were exhibited and offered for sale.... More than once I have seen a fire kindled in the Market Place, and fish sufficient to fill a cart which had been pronounced unfit for human consumption, heaped on the fire and burnt. From the Upper Borough Walls to Cheap Street was one continuous line of vendors. When evening arrived, some of these were lit up with naptha, some with oil and many with candles."

With a tradition of gentry trade, Bath was slow to catch the spirit of the retail revolution. A notable exception was the business opened in Union Street in 1870 by James Colmer. With its trade motto of "sterling value, small profits, no credit", it was "devoted to the requirements of the large residential population in distinction to the exclusive concerns of the Milsom Street region". In the space of forty years, Colmers (now Owen Owen) grew from its initial two premises to take over the space of nine shops on both sides of the street. Originally a drapers, Colmers' expansion, like that of Jollys, incorporated other trades to become a "tailors, outfitters and complete house furnishers" and so established itself as a department store. The emphasis on cheapness and high turnover featured in the firm's advertising. Not only did the store claim "the largest stock in the West of England" but the secret of success was: "Buying direct from the manufacturers, James Colmer Limited save the middleman's profit, the full benefit of which is given to their customers".

It was not until the Edwardian period that the familiar names of Boots appeared in Southgate Street and Marks and Spencers' Penny Bazaar in Stall Street. Old-style market trading continued to be popular amongst working class people even if its raucous style gave offence to respectable tradesmen complaining to the Watch Committee in 1894:

> "Mr. Alderman Bright, one of the Churchwardens of St. James's attended, and presented a numerously signed memorial from the inhabitants of that district complaining of the great nuisance existing at 19 Lower Borough Walls (where a person named Rufus Crook carries on his business

of Fishmonger and Meat Salesman) caused by his continual shouting and filthy language, the same being unfit for anyone to hear and also to the great obstruction of the thoroughfare."

Crook did a brisk business auctioning off his produce on a Saturday night before it became unsaleable. He evidently had a good line in vulgar, comic patter, the stock in trade of the stallholders at markets and fairs (last encountered at Twerton Market).

Ironically, we now see the large stores letting out space for specialist traders and Bath's continued prosperity as a shopping centre rests not merely on the big name stores but on the variety of its specialist shops, attracting a quarter of a million people who shop regularly in Bath.

What About the Workers?

"Bath has little trade and no manufacture, the higher classes of people and their dependents constitute the chief part of the population, and the number of the lower classes is small."

So wrote the Revd. Richard Warner in 1801, reflecting the predominant contemporary view and fostering the genteel image of the city considered vital for attracting visitors and new residents. Yet, in terms of size Bath was the eighth largest city in England in 1801 and as late as 1841 ranked eighteenth (equal with Leicester and Portsmouth) by which time it was too large to be sustained merely by seasonal trade. The prevailing economic activity in Bath was relatively small-scale compared with the great northern towns but it was not alone in this as the workshops of Birmingham and Sheffield testify. The major sector of male employment in Bath was in retail trade, frequently connected with workshop premises housing craft industries. While Bath proclaimed itself a place of resort and, later, residence for the gentry, it was increasingly becoming a centre of industry and commerce.

By 1831, adult males were predominantly artisans, masters in a small way, or in retail business on their own account, with a particular concentration in the central and southern districts of Bath. St. James's parish contained 12% of the city's male population but 28% of its tailors, 24% of its boot and shoemakers, 19% of its carpenters and only 5% of its domestic servants. A similar distribution occurred in female employment. A third of occupied women were domestic servants, mostly employed in the suburbs, while those engaged in the clothing trades as dressmakers and milliners, along with shoemakers, concentrated in the central parishes. Indeed, part of the large surplus female population of Bath can be explained by the employment opportunities in domestic service and service industries attracting girls from the surrounding counties.

By 1901, the building industry employed the largest single group of male workers, over 2,000 men and boys. Their lasting monuments are the suburbs that expanded the city dramatically in the late Victorian period. The largest development was of terraced artisan housing and of detached and semi-detached villa residences in Oldfield Park, the creation of local building firms and building workers.

Other flourishing industries in Bath were cabinet making and coachmaking. Cabinet makers, French polishers and upholsterers rose in number from 228 in 1841 to 342 in 1901 and those in coachmaking increased from 111 to 204 over the same period. Some of these small-scale enterprises were featured at the Great Exhibition in 1851, achieving a national recognition. Knight & Son were upholsterers to the Prince of Wales, their quality products being shipped all over Europe. Fullers, the carriage builders, had a large demand for their victorias in London.

New industries grew up alongside the traditional crafts — printing, bookbinding, and engineering. Pitman's printing business, founded in 1845, expanded to gain a national reputation through the pioneering of shorthand. Stothert and Pitt, the engineering firm, moved from its Newark Street works to a factory on the Lower Bristol Road. In 1851, the firm employed 540 hands and its cranes were to be exported to every continent in the world.

Allied to this industrial growth came an increased employment in various forms of transport. The opening of the Great Western Railway in 1841 and of the Midland Railway in 1869 brought new opportunities for employment as did the introduction of horse-drawn omnibuses later superseded by the coming of the trams. At Victoria's death, Bath had over a thousand men employed in transport. Reminders of these transport developments survive in the two railway stations and the old tram station, situated in Walcot Street.

The growth of new enterprises and the expansion of traditional craft industries was in response to the growing wealth of the nation. Dependence on local consumers and visitors lessened as the city's industry and commerce expanded. And as we have seen in our own time, new technology and improved industrial processes produced casualties in some industries. The numbers employed as tailors and shoemakers and unskilled labourers declined sharply in the second half of the century. Examples of declining industries are brewing, soap boiling and steam dyeing — all notorious for their offensive smells and all concentrated in the lower part of the city along the banks of the Avon. An old Bathonian, in recalling his youth, wrote:

> "The present inhabitants little realise the importance to the City of the trade in beer during the first 40 years of this century... The greater number of barrels were taken by special barges to Bristol docks, thence to Cardiff and Swansea for distribution to the miners in that region."

Pinchin's brewery in Northgate Street was reputedly the largest in the West of England with premises on both sides of the river, connected by a private tramway bridge. Soap boiling and steam dyeing were also carried on extensively. A large factory of dip candles for use in the mines and Marshall's Steam Dye factory were situated along Broad Quay. As river and canal transport became superseded by the railways, some local industries lost ground in the process.

Technological innovation and industrial change remains the pattern as Bath seeks a new prosperity with high-tech industry. The location of new industries close to the riverside belt of the old mills and breweries preserves historical continuity, and should serve as a reminder of Bath's industrial past.

A Healthy Image?

One of the benefits of a modern society is the provision of public health. Slowly and painfully, the idea of collective responsibility for the health of the community became accepted. The high mortality experienced in a series of epidemics gradually brought the common need to safeguard the health of all citizens to override individual interests and private property.

It began in earnest in Bath when in 1866 the city appointed its first medical officer of health, Dr. C. S. Barter. Two severe droughts in 1864 and 1865 and the worst epidemic of the century, when several hundred people died of smallpox in Bath, prompted the appointment. Even so it was a tentative beginning. The medical officer of health walked something of a tightrope. On the one hand, as a medically trained official, he was concerned with the health of the whole community; on the other hand, he was the servant of the council that employed him. Unwittingly or not, he was a public relations official as well as a medical officer of health.

*Dr. Brabazon: City
Medical Officer of Health,
1876–96.*

In 1867, Barter was clearly discomfited by a complaint that a false picture was being presented of Bath's sanitary condition in comparing the mortality figures of Bath with those of much larger cities:

> "In reference to some remarks that have been made in the Bath Chronicle respecting the Mortality Returns furnished by me," he noted in his report, "I beg to observe that it is impossible to obtain the numbers of deaths from any other towns than those published weekly by the Registrar General."

Public suspicion that a favourable gloss was put on the presentation of the figures was justified. The following month in Barter's annual report, he confessed that: "The death rate was high for a city like Bath" — a point repeated in later reports in which he argued strongly that Bath needed continuing sanitary improvement and a better water supply. Barter had one voice urging better health provision, adopted for the sanitary committee, and another in support of the healthy image of Bath, adopted for public consumption.

His successor, Dr. Brabazon, was even more willing to feed the growing sense of civic pride that thrived on self-congratulation. In the first year of his appointment in 1876, public criticism of the mortality rate in Bath provoked this comment in his report:

> "The apparent high death rate is considered an opprobium to our City, but the statistics of the week afford an easy explanation of the matter. I believe that in no city in England in proportion to population are to be found so many invalids suffering from *many + various* diseases, who come literally I may say to die.... but a pleasing note, more deaths above 80 are recorded in Bath, in proportion to population, than in any other city in England."

Yet two years later, Brabazon admitted that by comparison with the Registrar General's healthy districts, Bath had a higher infant mortality rate, "higher than it should be in Bath". At the same time, he referred to public criticism that his reports were manufactured to calm down public apprehension and indignantly refuted the suggestion. However, his annual report of 1878 gave the game away:

> "The city, judging from statistics, has been comparatively free from Epidemic disease of any type whatsoever, in such form as to create alarm. I trust this observation based upon the *published* facts will go forth to meet the eye of the public + particularly that portion of it, whose special avocation appears to be that of raising unfounded reports + injuring the *local + commercial* interests of this City."

Arguably, Brabazon identified himself too closely with the commercial interest represented on the Town Council which undermined his potential effectiveness in pressing for sanitary reform. Better public health required more public expenditure. Instead, Brabazon was inclined to blame high infant mortality on the ignorance of the poor. Improper feeding and neglect of health produced convulsions and atrophy causing unnecessary deaths. In the throes of a smallpox epidemic in 1879, he wrote: "I find it almost hopeless, the idea of impressing upon these people the necessity of strictly isolating the patient".

Certainly ignorance and intransigence went hand in hand but the poor, once provided with a Corporation water supply, brought the mortality rate down dramatically through improved cleanliness. The 339 deaths from typhus in Bath during the decade 1861–70 were reduced to just one death in the decade 1891–1900. Soap and water washed away the infected lice that spread the disease. More important still, the moral condemnation of "the great unwashed" was no longer tenable. It was a victory for the dignity of ordinary people.

Doss-House Shock Probe — The Avon Street Lodging House Scandal

This is a story of a night spent in an Avon Street lodging-house in 1887. An author from London, well versed in the conditions of doss-houses in the capital, disguised himself as a tramp, in the tradition of contemporary investigative journalism and revealed all to a startled readership of the *Bath Chronicle*. It caused a minor sensation. The author himself stayed in the city to address a public meeting and a flurry of letters followed the publication of the article which threw the council officials into a panic.

The story began in May 1886 when the Revd. Caulfield gave money to two young tramps to procure lodgings in the city. The next morning the boys complained of the overcrowded state of the room and Caulfield, as secretary of the Bath Vigilance Committee (for the detection and punishment of sensual offences), saw this as a golden opportunity to publicise the issue of overcrowding in the common lodging-houses in the city and the "moral evils" associated with their condition. Caulfield supplied the following "facts". The room in which the 2 boys lodged contained 11 people, although registered for five. Four of the beds were shared including bed no. 5 which contained a girl aged 20 and the two boys.

The proprietress of the lodging-house, when questioned, was prepared to verify on oath that there was no female present and a total of 4 men and 3 boys slept in the room in question, adding rather caustically "one of these two boys disappeared in the morning, forgetting to pay for the lodging, with the money kindly given by the Revd. Caulfield." This statement cast doubt on the veracity of the two young tramps. So more substantial evidence was required.

This was to be supplied in the new year 1887 when Howard J. Goldsmid, author of *Dottings of a Dosser* learned that "the Bath authorities had neglected to make bye-laws for the regulation of the common lodging-houses under their control." Goldsmid came down from London, by his own account, looking for damning evidence to use against the lodging-houses. He called on Caulfield, who furnished him with "a good deal of necessary information and proceeded to a lodging-house in Avon Street. His experience of the low "doss-kens" of London had taught him the necessity of disguise. So, dressed in "terribly old and ragged clothes", he arrived at the door of the lodging-house to be

> "accosted by a frowsy-looking specimen who desired to know what I wanted. 'Could I have a bed?' I asked and he

> motioned me to follow him into the kitchen where I stood
> by the door, while he, holding up a flaring tallow candle so
> as to give those present a good opportunity of scanning my
> features, repeated the question I had just asked him. 'Yer
> can 'av 'arf a bed,' said a puffy-faced, unsavoury looking
> hobbledehoy at the end of the room, and so having
> deposited 3d in his dirty palm I was duly accepted as a
> lodger.... The kitchen was fairly lofty, and had recently
> been lime-washed. It was, however, about as filthy as it
> could possibly be. There were eight or ten men there and
> one woman, a most slatternly creature, who smoked a large
> wooden pipe that emitted sufficient smoke to constitute an
> abominable nuisance."

Goldsmid made friends "with a big, red-faced man with dull, boiled gooseberry-like eyes, and a distinctly intemperate proboscis", who conducted him to a nearby establishment, half chandlers shop, half public-house. The room in this strange hostelry was very small and particularly dirty and unwholesome.

Having expressed a desire to retire, Goldsmid was ushered, through a filthy scullery across a yard, into an apartment, the door of which was marked No. 1. It was unusually lofty and well ventilated, but all the beds were double.

> "On the night of my visit there were only ten occupants,
> one of the beds being empty. As even with those ten the
> stench was well nigh unbearable, it is impossible to say
> what the atmosphere would have been like had the full
> complement of lodgers been present. The rugs and sheets
> were unusually filthy even for a common lodging-house.
> The vermin were many and active — to use the words of a
> song now heard in every pantomime in the kingdom — 'all
> very fine and large', and what with their incessant attacks
> and stentorous breathing of my very filthy and malodorous
> bedfellow, I was anxious to depart. But the enterprising
> proprietor had departed, locking the door of the lodging-
> house from the outside, and I was 'caught like a rat in a
> trap.'"

So there Goldsmid was compelled to stay until let out in the morning.

Goldsmid's account of his night spent in the lodging-house appeared next day in the *Bath Chronicle*. The very act of disguise encouraged the reader to share in an adventure exploring the territory of a hostile and alien culture.

Such descriptions were too obviously "colourful", owing much in appearance and speech to Henry Mayhew's London street characters of a generation before. So we are confronted by a "puffy-faced, unsavoury looking hobbledehoy", a "slatternly creature who smoked a large wooden pipe", and a "big red-faced man with dull, boiled-gooseberry-like eyes". All contain at least one adjective that condemns the conduct through describing the appearance of the person. And the images conjured up are almost too perfect as shock material that one suspects the use of artistic licence. Reaction to Goldsmid's article was immediate and indignant. The Revd. Caulfield was quickly off the mark in support and justifying his efforts in demanding that bye-laws be established to regulate the lodging-houses. A surgeon from The Circus echoed Goldsmid's demand for action. Conditions of over-crowding and uncleanliness were fertile sources of disease. And disease, he feared, could not always be guaranteed to select its victims from among the poor. Another letter-writer considered the vagrants beyond any help but was annoyed that adverse publicity would prejudice the commercial interest of the city.

Equally indignant were three residents of Avon Street. Mr. Baker, publican and shopkeeper, complained against "the mis-statements in Goldsmid's account".

> "No interior," he protested, "answers the description given — all are supplied with gas ... In justice to myself and neighbours, I feel it necessary to contradict Mr. Goldsmid and I am sure he writes on a subject of which he knows little or nothing in Bath whatever his London experiences may be."

Antonio Pierano, himself a lodging-house keeper in 84 Avon Street, equally felt compelled to contest Goldsmid's account, and added defiantly:

> "As regards my house, I invite inspection and will have much pleasure in showing anyone interested over it from cellar to garret. I should certainly expect to be prosecuted if there existed anything one quarter as that described by him."

The third resident, Mr. Gould, scathingly referred to the writer's "voyage of discovery" and called the account a "tissue of lies".

Under pressure from public concern, the M.O.H. investigated not only the lodging-house itself but Howard J. Goldsmid's book, *Dottings of a Dosser*. There he found comfort in that the graphic description of London Common lodging-houses was virtually identical to that applied to Bath. An inspection of No. 40 lodging-house at the back of Avon Street revealed that the room in which Goldsmid spent the night was licensed for 12 lodgers. The total cubic space was 4,658 cubic feet by measurement — an excess of 300 cubic feet beyond the requirement of the Model Bye Laws issued by the Local Government Board.

> "On the night in question," the M.O.H. continued, "I am informed there were 10 lodgers in this room in double beds + 1 single bed empty of which I am sorry Mr. Goldsmid did not avail himself. I have examined the beds + bedding + found no visible sign of the animal life vividly described in Mr. Goldsmid's accounts.... This is the unvarnish'd account of the apartment + premises as I find them.... I only wish the unregistered lodgings which are outside our control were as good + for which 2/6 a week is paid."

The final act in the saga of the Avon Street lodging-house scandal came in a meeting of the Sanitary Committee in February 1887. Discussion centred on the issue of new bye-laws. All the members agreed with the M.O.H. on the clean character of the lodging-house but the votes were in favour of passing new bye-laws. Alderman Clarke explained it by declaring it was better to pass bye-laws with a good grace than be compelled to do so by the Local Government Board. The reputation of the city was at stake. Fear of bad publicity that might frighten visitors and trade away meant the subject of Avon Street lodging-houses had to be suppressed. The private world of the transient poor was once more hidden behind the elegant facade of Bath's public image.

Suicide Row

While Victorian Bath projected itself as a genteel resort, parts of the city remained as no-go areas for respectable citizens. A magazine reported in 1852:

> "The visitor, however, is not to suppose that Bath is all beauty. On the low-lying lands on the bank of the river to the west there is a region of filth, squalor, and demoralisation, where poverty and crime lurk in miserable companionship, and where by a perversion of language, they may be said to enjoy, a kind of sanctuary free from the intrusion of respectability."

At the bottom of Avon Street and Milk Street, the New Quay formed an extension of Broad Quay that fronted the water as far as the Old Bridge leading into Southgate Street. Any illusion that this provided a pleasant riverside walk would be dispelled by the condition of the footpath, as reported to the Watch Committee in 1871, soiled by the practice of "persons constantly making use of the river path adjoining the Baths and Laundries in Milk Street as a privy." The whole quay area was a scruffy mixture of workshops, stables, warehouses, cranes and weighing engines. Industrial activity included stone yards, coachbuilders, maltsters, the Pickwick Ironworks and Marshall and Banks Steam Dye Works. Two pubs and a handful of cottages crowded in between corn factors, general carriers and a marine store dealer. This concentration of unsavoury activity alongside densely populated housing was reported in the *Bath Chronicle* in 1848 and attracted the attention of sanitary reformers:

> "Revd. Woodward referred to the offensive portion of the Quay, where sheepskins for parchment were exposed in order for them to become dry, inflicted on the opposite houses the nuisance of a slaughter-house."

Besides its economic function, the riverside area had a social usage. Opportunity was there for the curious or mischievous child to find something of interest. By day, the movement of goods always carried the possibility of petty theft. At night, a hay loft could provide shelter for homeless juveniles or for drunks incapable of making it home. A favourite pastime for the youths of Avon Street was to throw stones across the river. The pleasure in the collective sense of bravado made the more exquisite with the sound of breaking glass in the windows of Stothert & Pitt's engineering works on the far bank of the river. Younger children found their pleasure in climbing over and balancing on the sewage pipes which poured pollution into the river from the bottom of Avon Street. At low tide, there was a gap between the end pipes and the water to which children were irresistibly drawn.

A rather different attraction for youngsters in the late Victorian period was the annual visit of Wombwell's Menagerie, which found a temporary home in the open space to the Old Bridge. Lions and tigers held a marvellous novelty value in an age which had "discovered" Africa. Animal savagery may have found its mirror image among the wilder spirits of that riverside district. A rumour, only credible in such a context, was that children believed a man from the menagerie stalked the courts and alleyways at night with a big sack. As recalled by Bill Cottle of Corn Street, he was allegedly looking for stray cats and dogs to satisfy the voracious appetite of Wombwell's big cats.

A curious irony is that just below the Old Bridge, a main entrance to the city, lay the spot where the most desperate of its people took their leave, not just of the city, but of life itself. Here the melancholy scene beloved of Victorian novelettes was enacted. It was suicide row. The last wretched hours of those for whom life had become intolerable are recorded in the coroner's inquests. The following incidents took place in Bath in 1816:

> "David Price, labourer, gave evidence that he had known the deceased, 18 year old Franny Dayer, for two months: 'On Saturday evening last he was sitting in the kitchen at the Ship and Nelson in Horse Street (now Southgate Street) and she came in and drank with him. While there they agreed to go and sleep together. As they were going from thence to Avon Street along the Quay she complained her friends had behaved very ill to her in consequence of her going to Bristol with a man. They went to Mrs. Yearsley's in Avon Street and went up the stairs into a Room where she took off her clothes and sat on the bed crying very much. He asked what she was crying about but she would not tell him and said he knew nothing about her trouble. She continued crying and he told her if she did not leave off that he would go away. He was attempting to go when she said if he did not stay and sleep with her she would make away with herself. He went downstairs and she followed him as soon as she had put her clothes on. She was very much in liquor. They went down the street together and at the bottom of Avon Street as he was going home to the Ship and Nelson, he wished her goodnight and they parted. It was about 10 o'clock. She often talked of destroying herself. She appeared very uncomfortable about having left her friends and if it had not been for them she would not have been on the Town. She drank 2 glasses of rum and water, 1 glass of gin and water and a part of a quart of beer.' Franny Dayer, who had left home in Twerton only a few months before, was found drowned in the river Avon."

Each suicide represented a monumental human tragedy, usually featuring some ingredient of poverty, prostitution or drink.

The point of these articles, originally written for the *Bath Evening Chronicle* and entitled "Those were the days", is that Franny Dayer and suicide row are as much a part of Bath's history as "Beau" Nash or the Royal Crescent.